The Star-Brushed Horizon

The Star-Brushed Horizon

Don Gutteridge

First Edition

The John B. Lee
Signature Series

Hidden Brook Press
www.HiddenBrookPress.com
writers@HiddenBrookPress.com

Copyright © 2019 Hidden Brook Press
Copyright © 2019 Don Gutteridge

All rights for poems revert to the author. All rights for book, layout and design remain with Hidden Brook Press. No part of this book may be reproduced except by a reviewer who may quote brief passages in a review. The use of any part of this publication reproduced, transmitted in any form or by any means, electronic, mechanical, photocopied, recorded or otherwise stored in a retrieval system without prior written consent of the publisher is an infringement of the copyright law.

The Star-Brushed Horizon
by Don Gutteridge

Editor – John B. Lee
Cover Design – Sol Terlson Kennedy
Cover Image – Shutterstock
Layout and Design – Richard M. Grove

Typeset in Garamond
Printed and bound in Canada
Distributed in USA by Ingram,
        in Canada by Hidden Brook Distribution

Library and Archives Canada Cataloguing in Publication

Title: The star-brushed horizon / Don Gutteridge.
Names: Gutteridge, Don, 1937- author.
Description: First edition. | Poems.
Identifiers: Canadiana 20190076615 | ISBN 9781927725665 (softcover)
Classification: LCC PS8513.U85 S73 2019 | DDC C811/.54—dc23

For Anne
in loving memory.

Table of Contents

Part One;
The Star-Brushed Horizon

A Butterfly For Anne – *p. 2*
Affirmed – *p. 3*
Purveyor – *p. 4*
Jury – *p. 5*
Cadenced – *p. 6*
Reach – *p. 7*
Boys and Girls – *p. 8*
Fury – *p. 9*
Gender – *p. 10*
Stranger – *p. 11*
Millenium – *p. 12*
Unredeemed – *p. 13*
Roan – *p. 14*
Poverty – *p. 15*
Stippled – *p. 16*
Exalted – *p. 17*
Hamelin – *p. 18*
Wand – *p. 19*
Cyprus Lake: 1951 – *p. 20*
Hello – *p. 21*
Cyprus – *p. 22*
Felicity – *p. 23*
Stone's Throw – *p. 24*
Element – *p. 25*
Carnivore – *p. 26*
Solace – *p. 27*
Fisher – *p. 28*
Holy – *p. 29*

Night Skating – *p. 30*
Two for Mrs. Bray – *p. 31*
Lunar – *p. 32*
What We Are Called – *p. 33*
Impeccable – *p. 34*
Centennial – *p. 35*
Chances – *p. 36*
Dolly – *p. 37*
Speed – *p. 38*
Stamina – *p. 39*
Affable – *p. 40*
Other – *p. 41*
Foster's Pond – *p. 42*
Lost – *p. 43*
Blur – *p. 44*
Buoyancy – *p. 45*
Shinny – *p. 46*
Unravelled – *p. 47*
Warts – *p. 48*
A Kind of Light – *p. 49*
Anointed – *p. 50*
A World Away – *p. 51*
Roistering – *p. 52*
Incorruptible – *p. 54*
Cop – *p. 55*
New-Found – *p. 56*
Demur – *p. 57*
Pen – *p. 58*
Enduring – *p. 59*
Widow – *p. 60*
Astride – *p. 61*
Tug – *p. 62*
Art – *p. 63*

Struck – *p. 64*
Deke – *p. 65*
Miraculous – *p. 66*
Well – *p. 67*
For Anne – *p. 68*
Making Room – *p. 69*
Harry – *p. 70*
Enchanted Lake – *p. 71*
Non-Sense – *p. 72*
Desire – *p. 73*
Troubadour – *p. 74*
Glow – *p. 75*
Gist – *p. 76*
Tufts – *p. 77*
Season – *p. 78*
Boogie – *p. 80*
Ease – *p. 81*
Apostle – *p. 82*
Geronimo – *p. 83*
Dignity – *p. 84*
Honeycomb – *p. 85*
At Ease – *p. 86*
Beaming – *p. 87*
Sisters – *p. 88*
Random – *p. 89*
Swerves – *p. 90*
Goodbye – *p. 91*
Applause – *p. 92*
Only – *p. 93*
Orphan – *p. 94*
True – *p. 95*
Courage – *p. 96*
Bunny – *p. 97*

Shy – *p. 98*
Class Photo: June 1950 – *p. 99*
The Girls of Canatara – *p. 100*
Continuous – *p. 101*
Ballast – *p. 102*
Chairs – *p. 103*
Pedigree – *p. 104*
Odds – *p. 105*
Thrum – *p. 106*
Ashes – *p. 107*
Hope – *p. 108*
Dote – *p. 109*
Garden – *p. 110*
Couplet – *p. 111*
Career – *p. 112*

Part Two
Two Dozen For Anne

It is Hard to Believe – *p. 114*
In Lieu of Roses – *p. 116*
Loving You – *p. 117*
Mara's Lamp – *p. 118*
Not Any Gift – *p. 120*
Small Gestures – *p. 122*
Tears – *p. 123*
The Point – *p. 124*
Walking Together – *p. 125*
Urn – *p. 126*
Love Itself – *p. 127*
Locks – *p. 128*
Whatever Grows – *p. 129*
Kept Warm – *p. 130*
Endued – *p. 131*
Patient – *p. 132*

Marigold – *p. 133*
For Anne – *p. 134*
Coupled – *p. 135*
A Birthday Poem – *p. 136*
Cadenza – *p. 137*
Now You Are Gone – *p. 138*
Harmony – *p. 139*
Towards The Light – *p. 140*

Part Three
Another Poem for Anne

Crimson – *p. 143*
Always – *p. 144*
Harvest – *p. 145*
Epitaph – *p. 146*
Never Again – *p. 147*
Abiding – *p. 148*
Our Love is More Potent – *p. 149*
On Honeymoon Bay – *p. 150*
They Say – *p. 151*
Presence – *p. 152*
Urn – *p. 153*
Geyser – *p. 154*
Miss Barnett – *p. 155*
Humble – *p. 156*
Apart – *p. 157*
Nurture – *p. 158*
Beatitude – *p. 159*
Prompt – *p. 160*
Abrupt – *p. 161*
Eventually – *p. 162*
Pendulum – *p. 163*

About the Author – *p. 165*

Part One;
The Star-Brushed Horizon

A Butterfly For Anne
For Gerry Parker

You send this exquisite
green butterfly in lieu of
a visit, perched poetically
on an amaze of lines,
alabaster moons and a dazzle
of dots fancied afresh:
a master's art that says
how much you loved my Anne,
that utters its grief through
its breathless beauty.

Affirmed

After a reading at Mykanos
Restaurant in London, Ontario

There is a murmuring in the crowd
at Mykonos, all eyes
upon the ageing poet
as he grasps the lectern
and steadies himself under
the bright stage-light,
and, as those in their seats wait
to be wowed, words
drip off the bard's lips
in the sheer shape of poems,
rhymed or not, he reads
with surprising alliterative
ease, then nods at the sudden
outbursts of applause,
at the oohs and ahs in just
the right places, he smiles
a septuagenarian smile
in gratitude at something
significant having been affirmed.

Purveyor

For Ian Underhill

You spent a lifetime
purveying poems and stories
to generations of students,
reading aloud with alliterative
ease in your sturdy baritone
until the rhymes chimed
and the consonants collaborated,
until the metaphors stood
up and mentioned their meaning:
you gave them Munro and Purdy,
Atwood and Lawrence,
and all you asked for in return
was their passionate attention
and some small acknowledgement
that teachers, ungloried
as they are, really matter.

Jury

It's been a long and satisfying
life, and I intend to go
gently into Dylan's Good
Night: after all,
I've had my day, weaned
my soul from strife and woe,
eased myself into age
like a lark lifting into air,
content with what has been
allotted me, but the jury's
still out: as the last lick
of light flickers in the dark,
I may shout "Nay!" – bent
by bravado, fuelled by fury.

Cadenced

When Leckie's fallow froze
after January's thaw,
we took to the ice like ducks
on rudders, our blades scrolling
meridians we skimmed tenderly
under a moon hallowed
in the dark and a sky budded
with stars, boys and girls
together, hand-in-glove,
cadenced and going as the Earth
goes: we were all pluck,
ungendered, brimming
with hope and whatever
else comes before
the niceties of coupled love.

Reach

On sultry summer afternoons
we watched the wind-wafted
waves of Huron, as blue
as morning glories stroked
by lasering light, break
upon Canatara's
fabled beach, and we also
found time to cast
an unrighteous eye
upon the girls who once
were merely our chums
as they lay now full-
frontal on the sun-infused
sand, knowing all
along with our penultimate breath
that these creatures, lazing
there, feigning boredom,
would be forever beyond
our reach.

Boys and Girls

In the dallying darkness
over Monck Street,
under a monsoon
moon marinating side-
walk and roadway
with a mellowing light
and beneath Mara's luminous
lamp, we played out
our ritual games: Red
Rover, May-I
and most of all Hide-
and-Go-Seek, sallying
into the shimmying shadows,
waiting for the "All free!"
boys and girls alike,
where a knee might accidental
another, triggering a rush
of blood and a smile as big
as the star-brushed horizon.

Fury

How many summers did we while
away the days on Canatara
Beach, where the sun hummed
on the heat-soaked sand
and girls, new-breasted,
smile-beguiling and thigh-
shy, stretched out
before our salacious gaze
(hoping to be pursued perhaps),
but all we could do was shout
something rude
and plunge, unfazed, into Huron,
where we stroked each wave
with mammillary fury.

Gender

When Winter comes with its
numbing winds and crackling
cold, the swamp below
the village freezes tight,
and we on buoyant blades
are released from the vice-grip
of gravity for the seconds it takes
us to glide from west
to east like Vikings on a
silken sea, and if we,
emboldened, happen
to tumble backwards
into someone of the other
ilk (and inadvertently
tease a tender curve),
the ice will bear the blame
as we all surrender
to the pleasing ploys of the
gender game.

Stranger

When our dog Moochie
fell ill with distemper,
my father drove him into the
countryside and dropped
him off, and I've always
wondered what dog-thoughts
went whistling through his head
as, confused, dazed,
abandoned, he started up
the nearest lane, hoping
some stranger would call
out, "Here, pooch!"
and show him more love
than we did.

Millenium

These dunes are as old
as Methuselah's sire,
washed ashore by a thousand
wavelets tonguing the beaches
of Canatara, dried
by a thousand wave sifting
and enthusing the sun-
drenched sands into hummocked
hills that shimmered in the light
of the midsummer moon
and where, in an afternoon
of Junes, we played pirates
and thought of the Attawandaron
long ago greeting
the gods and the dream of dawn
and pressing their bent bodies
against the dune's drift
and listening to the millennial
hum of heat below.

Unredeemed

Above the hushed silence
of Cameron Lake, a menstrual
moon brushes the surface
with its tidal touch, and the woods
silhouetted with alabaster-
beaming birch are bereft
of birdsong except for Owl's
harmonized hoot, and the ink
of shadow within is sucked
shoreward to shrink
in the luminous wake where
loons abruptly rhapsodize,
and all seems tranquil
and true, while I stand
alone on the edge of everything,
fretful and unredeemed.

Roan

For Grace Leckie

I watched you galloping
across the fallow field
on your stalwart stallion
with a thigh-gripping ease,
and waited while you went
coursing by, your hair
bountiful in the breeze,
the roan tight-lipped,
nostrils a-flare, and I wasn't
sure whether I loved you
more, or the horse.

Poverty

When Moochie was just a pup
we couldn't afford to have
him take the shots that would've
prevented the distemper
he suffered, but instead
of letting him die among
those who loved him, my father,
to my alarm, drove him to the
countryside and dropped
him off at the nearest farm,
where I was certain he would
crawl to the barn and let
his life slip away,
alone and shivering, and I thought
how hard my father's heart
must have been, but then
by and by I had
another thought: my father
couldn't endure watching
Moochie die: even
so I still couldn't forgive
him for being poor.

Stippled

Nothing can retrieve
the aching days of my youth,
when I was unencumbered
by doubt, when the God I beseeched
to take my soul each
night before I slumbered
on safely through the night
routed my sins and follies,
and the sun unfurled
above First Bush
every morning and would do
so forever, and a
summering breeze strummed
the leaves of my grandfather's
maple with all the zest
of a jazz quartet, and I trod
the rippling streets of my village
ablaze with possibilities
of soothsaying and stories
stippled with truth, while Jesus,
pinioned and forsaken,
would rise again like Lazarus
and astonish the world.

Exalted

Loving you is an act
of remembrance, a recalling
of all those days when we were
too young to be tempered
by tactful touch or the soft
collision of lips, when being
amazed was our common fare,
when I knew such jolting
joy at a glimpse of your hair
haloed by juddering sun-
light or your eyes as blue
as crystallized cobalt
or the effortless allure
of your youthful gaze:
in truth our love was too
exalted to be nipped
in the bud.

Hamelin

For Jean McKay

You are a cross between
a pixy and the Pied Piper,
you move through the piebald world
on tingling tip-toe
the better to sense the myriad
oblong objects you trans-
mogrify with your singing
flights of fancy and dainty
dioramas; there is nothing too
small to fit your exquisite
eye, and all the while
you toss out flute
tunes, frenzied cadenzas
and a poet's prose to those
of us who love you
and are happy to follow you
all the way to Hamelin.

Wand

God, that great M.C.,
waved his magic wand
and Eden popped out of
the ether: a garden where tulips
and other blooms spawned
hither and thither until
Adam arrived, conjured
out of dust, to groom
the fruits and flowers and welcome
Eve, of whom he soon
grew fond, so that
when the slithering serpent,
in cahoots with Lucifer,
offered the Apple of Knowledge,
and Eve, grappling with temptation,
took a lusty bite,
Adam, pleased to assist,
and to spite his Maker, followed
suit, and the Lord, in a huff,
blew them both out of
Eden with a paradisal puff.

Cyprus Lake: 1951

There is no loneliness
like this lake, hedged
by cedars, birch and spruce
older than Adam's rib;
a lurch of wind induces
ripples on the silvering surface
that do not disturb the dark
deep where fish live
in soundless serenity,
and wavelets lick the stone
ledge where I stand
waiting for that first
word to propagate a poem
and set my bones aquiver.

Hello
For Tom

How many times
have we gone fishing
in the dolphin-blue depths
of Cameron Lake, where the sun
licks lavishly at the algae
blooms below and we peri-
granate for perch in the weed-
beds where minnows manoeuvre
out of their reach and I watch
the glow in your eyes as your line
jerks and, behold, a big-
mouth bass accelerates
up out of his habitat,
arched like a bent bow,
and you adjust your rig like a pro
and, hauling him in, you smile
and say, "Hello, that's
that!"

Cyprus

For my Uncle Potsy,
In Memoriam

The sun teetered above
the treetops as we motored
to the far end of Cameron
to the familiar creek, the sky
uncluttered by cloud
as we entered the mouth
in utter silence except
for an over-size bull-
frog plopping into the water
from a lily-pad with its little
nosegay of blooms
or grasshoppers vaulting
from ferns and fronds,
and thus we poled the boat:
me on the starboard,
uncle on the lee, our rhythms
synchronized, finding just
enough room for our caressing
craft, and then, at last,
storied Cyprus: pristine,
as blue as a morning glory
in a lash of light, un-
fished by any but we two,
encircled by birch
and spruce in every direction,
and the day passed without
a word to be heard
while we jigged and cast
and reeled in the odd
perch: a smile stealing
between us every hour
or so, strong enough
to seal the bonds of our affection.

Felicity

When I was fifteen and curiously
callow, I first laid
eyes upon Cameron,
my uncle's cottage and the birch-
bordered shoreline
hugging the water, bleached
blue by the sun's wilting
wattage, under which
black bass fed furiously
on paralyzed perch
and minnows undulated
in the shallows out of reach,
and we drifted in Cameron's
westering waves like dolphins
in a dream of felicity, and prayed
that this paradisal place
would always be.

Stone's Throw

The creek that links Cameron
and Cyprus meanders along
like an adder sodden with sun
slinking through the reeds
and water-lilies floating
flamboyant on the mirrored
surface, and from whose pads
bullfrogs leap
on their tantalizing trapezes
and land with a punctuated plop
in shallows no deeper
than an elf's ankle, and so
it is that we have to pole
ourselves from bend
to bowing bend, soaking
in the morning's saffron glow
and savouring the soul of this
perfected place a stone's
throw from Eden.

Element

I remember your first dip
into Cameron's shallows,
a tentative toe followed
by a slow progression until
your body was bottled in the Lake's
blue grip, and chest-deep,
without a by your leave,
you dive like a delighted dolphin
into the morning's supple light
and I breathe out again,
recalling with a sentimental
nod my own baptismal
plunge, and happy to see you
coupled by something
elemental, something
the Earth gave birth to
before it was born.

Carnivore

The odd time I've netted
a black bass in Cameron
I've wondered what it would be
like being a lunker, embodied
by water, unhorizoned
with eyes that do not
blink, even in sleep,
massively jawed to seize
each passing prey,
with no voice to converse
or utter pain or pleasure,
finned and gilled, perfectly
settled in this translucent
universe (no bigger
than a tarn), in which you are
both carnivore and god.

Solace

Everyone has a place
they go to, seeking
the solace of solitude:
it may as simple as a
rocker on the side verandah,
but for me it was Cameron
Lake, whose waters were the
hue of a bluebird's
breeze-brushed wing,
with a cottage mirrored in its
undimpled surface
and ringed by birches leaking
sunshine into a sky
as high and wide and deep
as the hushed horizon
my analogical eye perceived
just before the easing
of sleep.

Fisher

Only once did we find
ourselves in a feeding
frenzy on Cameron:
after an hour without
a nibble, rain began
to stipple the surface
and the fish started to bite
like barracuda on our worm-
curled bait, and soon
the bottom of our boat was paved
with squirming perch, their bellies
whiter than gouda, and suddenly
the sky turned blue
again, as insurgent breezes
played cadenzas on the rippled
waves, and oddly I thought
of Poseidon, god of the sea
and that other Fisher, of men,
who combed the shores of Galilee.

Holy

For Gran: In Memoriam

In Sunday School we sang
as if God Himself
were keeping tabs, while
back home my Grandma
baked her weekly raisin
pies and watched her Jello
cool in its bowl on the side
verandah: I found it odd
that the Divine seldom visited
our abode, but there was affection
in those prized pies and more
love abiding there
than the Lord needed to keep
His Sabbath Holy.

Night Skating

We go night skating
on Leckie's fallow in a static
snow, the kind that drips
from the lip of Heaven and parachutes
to Earth as soft as a lunar
landing, and the only sound
to break the serenity of the silence
is the soft heave of our breathing
and the whisper of flakes ecstatic
on the cheeks we hold aloft
like pilgrims awaiting manna,
and even though we are numbed
by the Arctic chill, we feel
as hallowed as we will ever
be in Kingdom Come.

Two for Mrs. Bray

Wounds

Bill Bray mowed
Grampa's 'back forty'
for fifty cents, half
of which he gave to his widowed
mother, whose clapboard
house was wombed with bloom,
and in there, amid
the daffodils and daisies
she grew happy, untouched
by war's wound.

Consolation

Mrs. Brays' wide-
brimmed hat floats
above the flowers she dotes
on (amid the hum
of bees) and gives no
sign of the sorrow she felt
at the grim news that made
her a widow, for these
creations, daffodil
or daisy, will have to do
for comfort and consolation.

Lunar

The moon gazed at itself
in the glazed mirror of
Foster's pond, and we zoomed
back and forth, shredding
our shadows, boys and girls
with tugged tuques and streaming
scarves, mittens just
shy of illicit touch,
and when someone yelled
'Crack the whip!" I found
myself tossed and flying
as sleek as a seal enticing
ice, while above all
the great Bridge loomed,
bisecting the sky
and arching towards the stars,
under which we skated
skittish and dreaming of
lunar love.

What We Are Called

To be given a nickname
was our town's way of saying
"Hello, you belong," and those
so honoured could be seen
whistling down Michigan
Ave and nodding to their sobriquet
as if it had been quickened
at birth, whether it was Rip
or Butch, Cap or Wiz
made no difference,
for a village is the Earth writ
small, the heart's home,
where no one is alone
and what we are called is as
deep as a knowing in the bone.

Impeccable

When Leckie's fallow glistened
like the mirrored pool of the Taj
Mahal under the auspices
of Venus and Mars, we take
to our skates and convene in ones
and twos beneath the jewelled
moon, the waltz of our wheeling
humming unschooled
in our heads, and the further we burrow
into the sheer shallows of the dark
we find ourselves listening to the
impeccable music of the stars.

Centennial

It wasn't the Santa Claus
Parade or even Macy's
Thanksgiving , but the brand-
new Fire Truck,
red as a raspberry,
led the way with the volunteer
crew hanging on
with both hands, followed
by the Boy Scout's
marching band, their bugles
blustering with all the zest
of a jazz ensemble,
and majorettes in their high-
stepping pace and twirling
batons glinting in the sunshine
the gods blessed us with,
and then came the vintage
autos, the Girl Guides
striding two by two,
a scuffle of ruffians from the
wrong side of the tracks,
and the Reeve in his rented limousine,
tipping his top hat
to the throng that lined Michigan
Avenue, and there was laughter
and tears amidst the merriment
and love for a town that had survived,
against the odds and with a little
luck, for a hundred years.

Chances

O the girls of the Point!
I see them now sifting
in the sunlight over
Canatara, their images
uplifted to my eighty-
year-old sight:
Nancy: as beautiful and un-
attainable as Guinevere
in some medieval romance
and I worshipped her from afar
like a lovelorn Lancelot,
and *Shirley,* just an inch
into her womanhood, stirred
in me feelings I later
learned were lust, and her sister
Betty, a big and bossy-
breasted Minerva who spun
the bottle and chortled at our
shy compliance, and *Joycey*
who longed to be Gaia
in her garden, but sported only
her underpants and puzzled
at the circumstances that left
her penurious and open to my
prurient glances: I see
them all again as clearly
as Huron's sky, re-anointed
by the years gone by,
and even now I'd like
to say: I like my chances.

Dolly

Dolly Gordon, after
an unfulfilling day
shovelling coal, liked
to quaff a beer or two
more than he should to ease
the pain and satisfy his soul,
but his good wife disapproved
of such indulgence, and when
he bent over, as far
as he was able, to clear
the cobwebs from his hobbled
brain, she tapped him once
on the skull with an iron skillet,
and when he woke, there was a
bulge on his bean, his head
was clear, and supper was on
the table.

Speed

When the ice on Leckie's fallow
was just thick enough
to bear the brunt of our blades,
we went flying down the centre,
eschewing the shallow edges
that broke like brittle glass,
and stroke by stroke we garnered
speed in gusts of sheer
momentum, until at last
we seemed freed from our body's
ballast and took flight
utterly into the air, as winged
as Icarus speculating on the sun.

Stamina

When the ice glazed the fallow
of Leckie's fields like the
sheen of moonlight
on a mesmerized meadow,
we skated out under
the auspices of the stars, young,
callow and gendered by choice,
our scarves fleeing behind
us like the wisping tails
of Halley's comet, and we felt
in our glistened gliding the tidal
tug of the universe and something
deeper than the stamina of the stars,
something unyielding,
hugging the bone, and leaving
us dazed, cloistered
and inalienably alone.

Affable

At the corner of Alexandra and Monk
Gran and Mrs. Bray
met most mornings
for their friendly chat and a laugh
or two, and the village being
both canvas and manuscript,
they talked about what
so-and-so said
to whom and other snippets
of this and that, tossed
out with a twinkle, until
the town grew round
and through them like a
dyslexic poem, pillaged
from the glossary of affable gossip.

Other

Shirley spun the bottle
with a wristed twist and stood
above our boy-girl
circle with lips at the ready
and bug-eyed with anticipation,
while I watched the jug spin
like Cupid's arrow, dread
in my heart as it whirled
through my neighbourhood
and stopped stark beside
me, and the girls whooped
as their gendered mate gripped
me by the waist and planted
one smothering, unchaste,
tongue-tender kiss
on my startled gaze, and I sensed
something other,
some joy grazing
astride, unthrottled
and three miles wide.

Foster's Pond

In the summertime we waded
big-booted into Foster's
Pond in search of cattails
we wielded like furred
tomahawks, and dreamed
of setting them ablaze
in the final fading of the day's-
long light, but in the winter
our pond glazed over
and we skated the afternoons
away, sailing like balloon-
rigged schooners among
the reeds and goose-grey
grass, lost to all
but ourselves in the fury
of speed and the blur of our blading.

Lost

Mrs. Bradley's mad
chatter could be heard
across our half of the village,
bruising the evening air,
disrupting hopscotch
and marbles, we paused long
enough to let our blood
chill and feel the intimations
of what it is to be old
and lost somewhere
in the mind you used to have.

Blur

After January's thaw
Leckie's fallow becomes
one great lake
unlinked to any horizon
and soon glazed over
and metamorphosed into a
rink without beginning
or end, and we found ourselves,
under a menstrual moon
in a sky as black as Dracula's
glance, skating on the iced
curves of the world, and girls
and boys with mittened fingers
in tentative touch in their
seesawing glacial glide,
and I kept one prurient
eye on the freckled face,
wind-nuzzled curls
and kittenish grin of the blur
beside me, whom I had fancied
since I first learned
what amazement was.

Buoyancy

Under a pale and translucent
moon and a sky scattered
with stars in their Grecian arcs,
we feel the bite of the ice
on our blades and cruise through the
hovering dark, glad
to be night-skating here
where the Earth has no edges,
and when Coop hits a shattering
of shale, we laugh at his pin-
point landing and his leveraged
leap upright,
and cheer when Marilyn spins
like a dulcimered doll, and Bonnie
and Sharon insist on doing
a duo as sisters, and Grace
and I come to the brink
of coy contiguity before breaking
asusnder, and the moon turns
as golden as a doting doubloon,
and we feel as a singular soul
the sheer joy of buoyancy.

Shinny

In the Winter on Saturdays
we played shinny on Foster's
Pond, with hand-me-
down sticks and a borrowed
puck, battered and burred,
and a goalie brandishing a broom,
like Turk Broda in his prime
(not even the catalogue-pads
so tenderly stitched
could undo his pluck)
as we skidded and slewed on the slick
surface in our galumphing
galashes, but we were young
and in the air above us
we could hear the skinny,
high-pitched voice
of Foster Hewitt urging
us on, while the crowd cheered
like Romans for the lions.

Unravelled

Oh, Nancy Mara,
I loved you always and from afar,
dreaming of warlike
knights and chargers barging
with a will through a hail of arrows,
along untraveled paths,
going for the Grail I would bring
to you to have your lips
sip its holy ambrosia,
or in another sally save you
from a life in serfdom
or worse, your gratitude
a lissome look was all
I needed as the blue igniting
of your eyes redeemed and endued,
till we danced in duo
upon the glistening sands
of Canatara before the thrill
of the tale unravelled
as dreams ever do,
and I, back on the straight
and narrow, was left still
loving you from afar.

Warts

My village was a three-steepled
town, and at precisely a quarter
to eleven each Sunday
morning, the Presbyterian bell
outrang its Anglican
cousin, calling the faithful
to people the pews, swell
the stalls and come forth
in the name of Christendom,
singing hosannas to the
high heavens, warts
and all.

A Kind of Light

When the moon bloomed as bright
as a galleon ablaze in a sky
littered with stars and their diamond
dazzle, we took to the ice
like Eskimos to snow, following
the girls, enwombed in wool,
who became just pals
for the night, skittering skillfully
over the glacial glaze
of Leckie's fallow, in un-
gendered duos or improvised
threesomes, our bodies
boneless in the winter chill,
wondering what it meant
to be and looking for the kind
of light we cannot see.

Anointed

Easter Sunday in the Point
was new shoes with the shine
still on them and pants
with a fine crease and ladies
bonneted and beribboned
and gentlemen in fresh habits,
and I remember staring at Christ
strung upon Golgotha (vinegar-
tongued, palms pinned
like moths on a lepidopterist's
display) just above
the altar where the Sabbath sun
limned His halo, and we felt
ourselves to be among
the anointed there, buoyed
by the yeast of prayer.

A World Away

When I was young and whiled
the world away in the midst
of my innocence, I ambled
around the village that bore
me up like a propagated
poem, unbeguiled
by anything "other"
beyond its mothering boundaries,
breathing the incense of its easing
air as I rambled wherever
I pleased over meadows
where milkweed pods
unfurled to dust the breeze
with providential puffs
and the wild mustard
flamed as golden as the
lustrous sun ripening
the snows that hung from their trees
like the appetized apples of Eden,
and even the thunder was muffled
there and the rains renewed
the grasses' bedizening and all
roads ferried me home
where love bloomed so
flagrantly no god
could sunder it.

Roistering

Each summer morning
the sun boiled out of
First Bush and layered
our streets with luminous light,
and I greeted the coming day
with a gallop and a prayer,
aiming my brand-new
body towards the doors
behind which the friends
who drew me outside
of my centering self
awaited my hithering call:
Wiz Withers whose magical
hands could weave gizmos
and gadgets out of anonymous
odds and ends with a kind
of ledgerdemain even
the gods envied:
Butch McCord who had
no other name
but cushioned the blows of bullies
just for me, who trod
the voluminous girders of the Bridge
to show the world what daring
was and what it meant
to be a brother:
Jerry Mara who could swim
like a perambulating porpoise
and carried our daily play
to Canatara and beyond,
who gave full meaning
to the word loyalty:

Bones Saunders all
elbows and angles,
who let us stick him
with a nickname and hoisted
the friendship flag:
and so it was I learned
like Adam before the fall
what love was, its synesthetic
edge, its numinous glow,
and before the gloaming loomed
we all went out and royally
roistered..

Incorruptible

On soft summer mornings
the sun rises up out of
First Bush like a Phoenix
pouring Grecian light
on the village streets below,
and we are released like
Moses out of Egypt into
the airy outdoors,
and it's Move-Up in Withers
field, hopscotch
or Double Dutch with the girls
gliding aloft and a-glow,
or ring-around-a-rosy
with the little'uns in tow,
or, on a good day,
when bees hum to hear
themselves sing,
surprising Wiz in his cellar
with his magical gadgetry,
and we are as free as leaves
unleafing from the density
of the tree, and insulated from the
burst of the world by our
incorruptible innocence.

Cop

Our village had but one
cop, few villains
and even less trouble:
Constable Pedan, whose principal
task was scouring the alleys
to get a bead on truants,
stopping the odd jay-
walker on our carless
streets, parsing the Pool
Room for underage
felons, rousting un-
ruly hoboes
from their afternoon snooze,
guiding to hearth and home
gentlemen who'd imbibed
too much booze,
or pursuing Butch and me
riding double and beating
his flat-footed trot
to the Bridge, where we hid
below its looping span,
pleased with ourselves
and basking in our own glow.

New-Found

The wood-burning furnace
below heaves its heat
up into the classroom
above, where twenty-three
pupils in eight grades
sit rapt and waiting
for Miss Nelson to blow
into her pitch-pipe and tweet
a perfect "cee", after which
we all sing our anthem
to the King, and school begins:
that's me in the middle row
(good at reading but little
else) glancing across
two aisles at Grace
and indulging in the bulge
of her new-found breasts:
she fails to turn around,
and I am seized with some-
thing akin to despair,
uncaressed by hope,
watching her face pointed
straight ahead, her tresses-
enriched by the morning
light, at ease, alas,
with her womanhood.

Demur

Joycee Clark was rumoured
to be promiscuous,
but not knowing for a fact
the meaning of the term, we had
to be content with wishing she'd
drop her pants and do
the hula-hula dance,
and then surprise us all
by showing off the tender
cleft between her thighs
(we dreamed the daylights
out of), but what we got
instead was a demur purr
and a furtive smile that left
the mystery intact.

Pen

I took up my pointed pencil
at Grade Three, not
knowing what odd urge
took hold of me,
but I recall the surge of serenity
as the blank page came
alive in my eyes and the
surprise that stories were born
inside before they aged
and allowed themselves
to be written and read,
and I knew even then
it wasn't for renown or glory
but the release of words in their
anointed wonder on the chance
that someone disembodied
out there might understand
and give me the nod:
I can't tell you or God
when, but the time will come
when I will have lain down
my pen.

Enduring

Gran was always good
for a nickel; I can still
hear the crisp click
as she opened her purse and lifted
a shiny five-cent
piece onto my outstretched
hand, and then it was off
to Harry Brand's (with his eighty-
year, tight-fisted
smile) for a Pepsi (sucked
till the straw gave up)
or a couple of grab-bags
or a pair of black-balls,
and I thought then, as I do
now, how lucky I was
all those years to have
such a grandmother and the enduring
gift of her love.

Widow

Mrs. Bray floats
among her flowers, swallowed
by sunshine, and glides
through her sea of petals
like Gaia on a good day,
doting on daisies or roses
and loving the way light
laps at the lips of poppies
or black-eyed Susans,
the way her garden grows
effusive, reminiscent
of that other garden
where there were no
wars and no widows.

Astride

For Sharon, Bonnie and Marilyn

The girls gather round
Marilyn and the pony she sits
astride, buffing the pommel
with her free hand, as `Sharon
strokes the curling mane
and Bonnie giggles as Champ
pokes his nose into the
feed-bag, and the sisters
beg for a ride they will never
own, while in the fallow field
the stiff-legged hired
man hobbles homeward,
roughshod and randy.

Tug

The girls are hopscotching
bare-legged in the breeze,
skipping from square to square
with the elegant ease of an acrobat
on a tremulous trapeze, while the boys
in the field beside them
are tossing a rugby ball
with the ardent thrust of a right
arm, watching its awesome
arc all the way
home, while the girls squeeze
their thighs tight in their high-
wire flight, and the boys
dream non-stop
of touchdowns and the tug
of desire.

Art

This is me at nine
months, the photo craftily
coloured to bring out
the bloom in my cheeks and the sweet
green of grandfather's grass,
and who knew what plots
and stanzas lay behind
that unblemished brow
(the sorcerer's art
with words perhaps) or what
poet's passion I might
unfurl some day
and startle the world.

Struck

The things I remember:
five-year-old
Tom, tucked a-bed
and trying not to sleep,
his eyes still beaming,
alive with expectation,
and me alongside,
singing "O the great
ships sail through the
alley-ally-O
on the first day of September"
until, soporific with song,
he drifts into some dream
I am not privy to,
and I too begin to doze,
struck once again
by how deep love
goes.

Deke

Sarnia City Champions
1933-1934

I sit in my solitary study
and notice an eighty-year-
old plaque once
held in my father's hands,
and I see him skating
as sweet as a swan on the
magic mirror of a pond,
his dekes and yaws as smooth
as new ice on a raw
rink (he has the boy's knack
but the puck-wit of a pro)
and I can hear the applause
of the home-town fans
who made this slim kid
their hero, and what joy
it must have been to feel
every breath in your body
tuned to the grace of the game,
and no hint then
of the grim days ahead
when he was no longer
slim and, done in
by drink, couldn't out-
deke Death.

Miraculous

In the midst of my fever I saw
diaphanous-winged angels
fluttering like butterflies
just before bidding
farewell to their cocoons,
and singing a Siren song
as they gestured me gracefully
towards Heaven, where no
fevers thrive and there is
no need for the future,
but something gut-deep
and bracing in the bone drew
me back, and I awoke
to a welcoming, miraculous moon,
sweating and alive.

Well

Sometime soon
the last person to recall
my name will have just
forgotten it. But
for all those at whom
I have hurled my misanthropic
thoughts and rhyme-riddled
dreams through the prism
of my poems (that promised
more than words are allowed
to tell), please, remember
me well.

For Anne

If you were a flower you'd be
a yellow rose sweetening
sunshine on June
afternoons, and at the edge
of evening mellowing moon-
light: we greet each
other in the morning's rise,
empowered by love in the
other's eyes, watching
as it grows and blooms
over the long years
we have been buoyantly
embowered.

Making Room

We love to watch our grand-
children grow, galvanized
by their preordained ages:
infant, toddler,
pre-schooler and teen,
and so engaged are we
in the world we barely notice
the ticking of time, but each
year they add is one
less for us, groomed
for demise, making room.

Harry

For Katie and Rebecca

My granddaughters devour
Harry Potter, un-
daunted by the tome-thick
prose; they are at home
with the wizard and his
necromancing tribe,
absorbed by story itself
and its passionate action,
fuelled by just the right
flight of fancy, each
word newborn
in the mind's might: they
consume books with a
gustatory delight.

Enchanted Lake

It lies a bejewelled blue,
this lake that fueled
my boyhood imagination,
(I pictured lissome fish
and whales sailing) where
the uncle whom I loved
like a second father and I
trolled for trout or. on a
lucky day, a big-
mouthed bass who might spit
the hook and billow away
into the gleaming underworld
below, and on soothing summer
evenings we would swim
like breath-spent porpoises
in the shallows were a million
minnows mirrored the shrunken
sun as it shimmered between
the prisms of spruce and cedar
that circumscribed my Cameron
and endowed it with a shape
that glimmered through my dreams.

Non-Sense

There is something of the
mad in every poet,
a tinge of intranquility
in the mind's dark density,
a dis-ease in the iambic
where the imp in impious
quivers the bardic quill,
and should pentameters flow,
they do so better
when radical, unhinged
from sense.

Desire

When God ripped Eve
out of Adam's ribs, what
he saw was a mirror image
of himself: with breasts
unsuckled and an extra
cleft and hair that hung
like flung flowers; he felt
no fire in his loins
as hand-in-hand they strolled
the groomed sod, until
Eve purloined an apple,
and Adam, smitten, came
unbuckled with desire.

Troubadour

Leonard Cohen is dead,
that sonorous deep-growled
thrum forever stilled;
he took a sound embedded
in the bowel and raised it
through his poet's throat
to haunting song (while
in his verse he played the minstrel
with a magic, whimsical wand);
there was always something
of the dirge or lasering lament
in the willfulness of his lyric,
in the tragic timbre of Hallelujah,
he gave us more than
we thought possible in the human
voice: this troubled,
talented troubadour.

Glow

My girls are like the glow
that roses make when bussed
by the summering sun under
a moonless sky and no
clouds above to brush
the bountiful breeze aside,
with eyes alight and wide
with wonder they brighten every
room they sidle into,
like poppies blushing crimson
in June: I never grow
accustomed to their levitating
love.

Gist

Whenever Mara's lamp
blinked into the inked shadows
of Monk Street, we gathered
boys and girls together
like guineas round a fist's
throw of oats in the June-
lewd sun, savouring
its lascivious light under
a sky stamped with stars
and a monastic moon floating
in the black above, and we
re-enacted the age-old
rituals with ampled exactitude,
while thinking of our afternoons
on the dune-rich sands
of Canatara and its erotic
urges, and needing no
reason, purging or exotic,
to question our right to relish
the joyful gist of the seasons.

Tufts

On winter evenings when the snow
sifted down on Monk
Street like the silken tufts
from milkweed pods
and a hazy moon caressed
the flakes that kept our god-
less games aglow,
we thought of Bethlehem
and shepherds in the muffled
air over Galilee,
and we peered at the tingling
sky above, looking
for a single star to ignite
the larcenous night and cast
some bountiful blessing
upon our All Free!

Season
After John B. Lee

We were all at ease with Autumn,
when everything green
in McPherson's orchard
turned as rosy as a bride's
blush, and we bit into the fruit
and let the exotic juices
glide chinward,
and dreamed of apple cider
and the acrid edge of its aroma,
and in the swamp that hugged
the Point, bulrushes and cattails
flourished, furred and dappled
in their dying, and the maples in our
yard reddened before
their fiery fall, and along
the road to our country school
the ditches were rich with golden-
rod that summoned sunlight,
and the mist-teased fields
festooned the air with the florid
fleece of wild carrot
and dilatory daisies, and later
on, the pungence of moon-
rounded pumpkins split
wide and oozing pulp,
and winter wheat whisking
furrows, like peach-fuzz
on the chin of those

seeking to leave behind
the tug of childhood:
being young we cared
not that Autumn was, at bottom,
the season of root-rot
and dank decay, for ours was a
world where hope had its say.

Boogie

At a quarter to noon we stood
breathlessly on our walk
and waited for Herbie Gilbert
to sail by in his almost
new Tin Lizzy
and waited for the grin as he
bassooned the ooga-ooga
horn and thrilled a neighbourhood,
leaving them dizzy with delight
and letting us know that being
happy was as easy as being
adult with a Model T,
and we dreamed there on our
home curbs of doing
the boogie-woogie until
the future failed us.

Ease

Shirley: lying on the beach,
and I try not to watch
as her thighs ease innocently
open, undeterred
by the tight tuck of her one-
piece bathing suit,
or, delighted with my luck,
stare in my boyish
bravado at the winking wrinkle
where her crotch catches
the luminosity of Canatara's
sun, and what I feel
is less than desire and more
than curiosity, for I am
the intruder, Eve's adder,
reaching towards something
teasing and untouchable,
impatient in my prurience.

Apostle

For Grace Leckie

My mother called it "Puppy
love," but what I felt
had nothing to do with dogs
before their dotage: my body
refused to breathe whenever
you glanced my way, oozing
some intimation
of romance that left me
utterly bereft of speech,
and when you and your stallion
stutter-stepped past
our house a mile beyond
my reach, my heart, jostled
ajar went hectic
at your angelic smile,
like an apostle at the Last Supper.

Geronimo

The dunes of Canatara are infused
with the heat of a thousand suns,
tiny infernos festooned
with tufts of grass livid
since Adam left Eden,
and soon to be our make-
believe mountains where cow-
pokes out of cahoots with the law
take cover, waiting
for the adamantine dark
to cool their six-gun
itch and a moon above
pitching its glacial glow
upon a boy like me,
playing Geronimo.

Dignity

When I was still young
enough to wonder at the world,
I would watch each morning
Ol' Cap Garvey
shuffle past our gate
en route to the mail
with his skipper's dignity intact,
and marvel that his hair had turned
snow-white after
the storm of 'thirteen when waves,
unmuffled by the seething
winds, sent dozens
of lakers under, and I thought
about what it would take
to keep that malignant
memory alive for seventy
years.

Honeycomb

The bees in Mrs. Bray's
groomed garden tremble
on the tingling tips of stamens
tossed here and there
by a playful breeze, and probe
with their buzzing proboscis
deep into the nectared heart
of a tulip or rambling rose:
they've mastered the art of pollination,
and before cruising to their honey-
combed home, they leave
behind a dozen blooms:
bee-blossomed.

At Ease

When I was young and free
and at ease with the world,
every morning was a superb
surprise, as the sun up-
rose above First Bush,
inking it with Apollonian
light, igniting the trees
elder than Eden and shimmering
shade where robins throbbed
with song, and Huron Lake
was wave-wakened and generous
enough to swallow Heaven
whole, and grandfather's yard,
laddered with lilacs, opened
to my impatient eye and welcomed
me into its paradisal precinct,
for there were no adders
slithering silkily through my garden
in search of Eves and apples
that hung like pendulous prizes:
for I was young and the world
had yet to be unfurled
and hence was I pleased to harbour
its hithering to-and-fro
with my incorruptible innocence.

Beaming

Gran would take me to the
Band Tattoo in Athletic
Park because Grandpa couldn't
stand the tuba turbulence
or the trumpeting turmoil,
but we loved the skirl of the
kilty band, the tremulous
tooting of horns, the tinkle
of the glockenspiel, the glacial
glide of the trombones
and the smart marchers stepping
stride for stride: the teeming
maelstrom of music
I adored because Gran
was beaming at such guilty
pleasure and what-is-more
she was sitting beside me.

Sisters

Betty was the big sister,
boasting breasts and a blistering
tongue, Shirley was all
cartwheels and flexibility,
flipping hither and yon:
we hung about their yard
like puppies in need, playing
spin the bottle with chaste
kisses and hesitant hugs,
but when Betty loomed,
the air grew greedy
with something unthrottled,
slithering and serenely sexual.

Random

It was in Bill McCord's
rink that my Dad's story
was first written, where he skated
with the inborn grace
of a swan over the silken
face of a perfect pond,
where he thrilled his rabid
fandom with deft dekes,
brisk bursts and mad-
cap dashes – until the day,
while they were building the bridge
that would loom over the town
like a rectilinear moon,
a red-hot rivet
without a nod or a pivot
dropped straight onto
the roof of Dad's arena,
burning it to ashes,
and though I was barely proof-
read, I must have thought
there are things in this world
that are random.

Swerves

Shirley McCord was our
mate, flipping cart-
wheels on grandfather's
much-mowed lawn,
skipping Double Dutch
or playing hopscotch
May I? and, when a bit
risqué, Post Office:
we made the most of our joint
childhood, (our days
unbordered) but when,
after an absence of two
years, I spotted a girl
on Canatara, all
swerves and curves and pertinent
points, my heart hopped,
unsure how it
should feel, and when she said,
"Hello, Don," I wished
for a slow moment that Time
had stopped when we were young
and certain of the way the world
would go.

Goodbye

"I'm on the road to recovery,
Donny," were the last words
my grandfather spoke
to me, before the sutures
broke and he bled to death,
and to keep my spent spirits
lifted, I dreamt of a dozen
farewells when the future
we shared had come to a close:
breath on breath, our heads
held high, and savoring
the gift of goodbye.

Applause

There I am seated on the
railing of grandfather's
side verandah, reading
my maiden "epic" to an audience
of three: the McCords and my pal
Butch: my words greeted
with only a touch of the skeptic
and more surprise than I
thought warranted, my voice
just failing to reach
the authorial tone I aimed
at (with a pregnant pause
or two), and I waited in vain
for the applause due to the
uninhibited, juvenile
scribe who dared to perpetuate
his plots on the pages of a
ten-cent scribbler.

Only

On the mile-long trek
to our country school, boys
and girls in a straggling gaggle,
we passed Leckie's pasture
and cast our eyes on the young
colt there, his roan
coat surprised by a morning
sun, set on the horizon
ahead like a gilded marigold,
and below the colt's belly
hung a bright red
erection, throbbing like a
bruised thumb, as the girls
went numb with shock,
looking in every direction
but Leckie-ward, and we
boys locked our gaze
on the proud protuberance
and considered something
other than romance and moons
on star-startled nights:
the furious fusion of that
amazing instrument with another
receptacle we couldn't quite
fathom, as the girls giggled
and Coop broke the spell:
"That's only his pecker,"
he smiled.

Orphan

Aubrey Lyttle was adopted
by our elderly neighbours
after four bleak years
in an orphanage with no takers,
but his luck turned at last
and he found himself
with what he wanted above
all: to be loved, to be
entitled to a name he could
boast about, to have
parents who would see to
his niggardly needs (we welcomed
him into our gang as our mascot,
we admired his curls and boyish
pluck) and all was well
until his new father died
and his new mother sent
him back to the place where
joy was in short supply:
after all these years
I still think of Aubrey,
and my heart still bleeds.

True

When the world was young in my
infant eyes and the sky
was ablaze with blue and grand-
father's lawn was as green
as grass after a rain
and the lilac hedge that edged
my docile domain bloomed
like a bride's bouquet
and the spirea that hugged my northern
border feathered the air
with its flowers and every stick
and stone was a superb surprise
and I ventured warily into the wide
outside, tethered always
to the known and true: at home
in my bones.

Courage

For my Grandfather: in memoriam

These yellowed medical
records tell the story
of your suffering and affliction
(two wounds and dysentery)
but make no mention
of the courage it took to breathe
in the rat-riddled mud
of trenches or to pick lice
out of your fellows' hair
or fling yourself into
No-Man's-Land
singing with bullets and the cries
of the dying and the silence
of the dead (knowing there was no
glory in the blood and mire
of battle), or the courage to enter
sleep each night
not certain your dreams
might be your last, but
I like to think your final
thoughts before exhaustion
claimed you, were about
the possibility of a future
free of combat,
and one that included me.

Bunny
Easter 2017

At Eastertime the magic
bunny hopped from room
to room depositing eggs
and other treats under beds
and commodes, where we,
pleased to be teased,
discovered them without
divine direction, and then
it was off to Sunday School
with new shoes and a heart
heightened by news of the Resurrection,
with Jesus somehow
finding the strength to roll
the stone away from his three-
day tomb and levitate,
turning a tragic story
into a tale primed with God's
glory and one honey
of a bunny.

Shy

For Bobby Cooper

Shy doesn't do justice
to the diffident dignity
you offered the world, but
there was a twinkle in your eye
that betrayed the elfin imp
inside, who kept Belgians
in a hutch next door,
while we watched their noses
dimple pink; we spent
long days on Canatara's
sands on the brink of Huron,
where westering winds under
the simple sun gusted
the waves we leapt in tumbling
tandem; here in your class
photo you stare at the ground
as if the camera might expose
more than you were willing
to present to us who loved
your humble humor and all
that friendship you bestowed
on me for four short
years, whether I deserved
it or not: we plotted
our future together
and dreamed, as the days went by,
that it would never end.

Class Photo: June 1950

The sepia tones now
just a little faded
in this photographic sketch
that freezes time's fallacious
flow: the classmates
I knew so well:
Bobby Cooper who raised
rabbits in a hutch next
door and watched their noses
wrinkle pink, Ronnie
Young who tried to lick
the moon off the boys'
window, Bonnie and Sharon,
queens of Double Dutch,
Donnie Turnbull
who clutched our rugby ball
like a lover's squeeze, and his cousin
Moo Cow Margaret
we teased until we teared up
in shame, and front and centre
my dog Moochie posed
for his portrait, and Miss Nelson,
who taught us to love
what we learned, and all those
other faces I can name,
as if the years in their yearning
had not intervened:
I feel the tug of remembrance;
memories are etched in the runes
of our bones.

The Girls of Canatara
For Nancy Mara

The girls of Canatara
cavort on my beach
like gazelles grazing
the grass-tops of some
vast savannah before
they sprawl splendidly
on the satisfying sand,
where we gaze on the curves
and swells of their bountiful bodies,
on the sassy swirl of their curls
and on the gifted grace of their
unpinched faces, knowing
full well we were not
the sort to raise an eyebrow
or solicit a sigh, or bring
a girl like Nancy Mara
one inch closer
to my ravenous reach.

Continuous

The geography of my village
is a memory-map lodged
in my mind's eye forever,
but when I venture back,
I am baffled by the distance
between by-gone and be,
puzzled by the chasm between
was and is, has-
been and hope, where the streets
are hodgepodge and the houses
awkward and askew,
and it's only when I come in sight
of the Lake with the sun hefted
upon its copious blue
horizon and the sinuous sands
of Canatara that I feel
upright, assured of a world
that is continuous, that will be
here long after me.

Ballast

You have only one home:
having weathered the womb
and the burst of birth, you greet
the village that envelops you whole:
first, there's grandfather's
lawn, lavished with lilacs
and foaming spirea with a yard
yawning enough for a dozen
LaSalles to explore, and soon
a street teases a granny-
cracked sidewalk and an ally
blooms where pals pop
up and fraternize, and both
of your feet touch the Earth
until a song sings
itself to your soul: of ballast
and belonging.

Chairs

On cloudless afternoons
when the humidity allowed
or the sun didn't scorch,
you would sit on the front porch
with a good book and an extra
nook for a neighbor to stop
by for a friendly chat
about this and that or any
news stimulating the street:
there was no fuss
or fume about you, you spoke
your many kindnesses aloud,
you thought from the heart, and despite
my earnest prayers, I look
out now and what
I see is two empty
chairs.

Pedigree

Out favourite cat, Peachy,
proud of her feline pedigree,
brings us a gift, a robin
tangled in her teeth, its red
breast still aglow with the
living sun, a song
no longer throbbing
in its throat, and the tabby looks
up beseechingly as if
expecting (above all)
a pat on the brow that would make
her purr like a sated lover.

Odds

If there's a Heaven you'll be
first in line, your kindnesses
are heroic in a wayward world
where they are few and far
between, and when good
deeds were assigned in some
celestial lottery, you took
your share and much of mine,
and most of all you chose
to galvanize your love
for one who hopes, against
the odds, that Paradise awaits
and there really is a God.

Thrum

It begins with a thrum in the blood,
something marinating the mind
before becoming an itch
that hitches itself to a word,
perhaps even a kind
of phrase, fully framed,
that tickles and tantalizes
until it sticks in the rut
of a rhythm, surprised by
sense, a semblance of meaning
straightened by metaphor
and the sibilance of simile,
by the extravagance of stanza
and a line's elastic dance –
and thus does a poem give birth
to itself and the Earth tilt
an inch on its axis.

Ashes

Another Mother's Day
and still I think of you
as the callow girl who must
have fallen for a fellow who skated
with the grace of Gordie and the panache
of Rocket Richard, who tingled
the air above the local
rink in front of you
and the adoring crowd, when I
was not yet thought aloud,
when love was all it seemed
to be, a plot to fix
the future's fate and your life
had not yet turned to ashes,
leaving me without
a day to celebrate.

Hope

For Nancy Mara

I sit in the sand and watch
Nancy dive, in the air
elegant as an antelope
holding its breath, she whispers
the water with barely a ripple
stirred, her lissome limbs
vanishing, saying goodbye,
and leaving me, a non-
swimmer, crippled by shyness,
without hope.

Dote

For Tim and James

I dote on this photo:
James and Tim rudely
nude, posing on my easy
chair and feeling quite
pleased with themselves,
their multiple cheeks as rosy
and cheerful as cherubim
in an angel's arms, and I thank
whatever god brings me
such gifts that raise
a smile and lift the farthest
valves of the heart.

Garden
For Beth Whitney

I walk by your garden
and there you are, encircled
by the blooms you talked into being
with the same syllables Eve
must have used on the first
flowers to flourish in Eden:
you've found room
in your gardener's heart for
daffodils and daisies,
roses and their cousins that tickle
the air with their technicolour
flair and bring the neighbours
more delight than a dozen
rainbows or stars
that startle the night.

Couplet

This life, such
as it is, (all tremor
and tentative touch)
may be summed up
in a single couplet:
we worship whatever thrives
and mourn the abrupt brevity of our lives.

Career

I try to imagine the day
when I'll write my last line
of verse on the uninked
page; will it be a simile
that sings like an oriole's aria,
a metaphor succinct
in its mirroring magic,
or perhaps a rhyme to startle
with its simple chime: in any
case I shall lay down
my pen with a Chanticleerian
cheer: calling it a career.

Part Two
Two Dozen For Anne

*For Anne, the love of my
life, in loving memory*

It is Hard to Believe

For Anne: Christmas, 1996

It is hard to believe
we are growing old:
June upon June the dark-
eyed daisies irrupt
jubilant and anew
from the wrinkled root you
long ago cupped
in your bride's grip and
persuaded into the earth.

Once again you stand
sturdy and watchful
among the tendril'd bloom
of iris, dahlia, sweet
william, who bend up
to your touch like children
anticipating praise or,
like you, listen merely
for the winter note under the
honey-buzz of pollinating
bees, the sound the world
makes when all the robins
hesitate…

But: mother,
lover, husbander of so many
green things that must begin,
you turn your face towards me,
lay a plucked petal
along your open throat,
and — as the shastas / blood-
root / cosmos / flox
shimmer at your sandalled feet
and bear you bodily aloft
like some remembered Persophone
in the hour of her element —
your smile brindles the aging
air as it did the first
day I beheld its burst
among the bursting flowers.

In Lieu of Roses

Valentine's Day, 2006

Snow on Valentine's Day,
a hush heard in the heart,
but love blooms anyway
and we, separate or apart,
find room for each other,
summer on what we recall
of June and the seasons shared:
Spring and snow-free Fall
(and Winter, too, one supposes).

Oh, I need no rhyme or reason
to send you this poem's love
in lieu of a dozen yellow roses.

Loving You
For Anne

Loving you is as easy
as breathing, and our long
lives have not diminished
the intricate dance of our
separate selves, and above
all else we touch
each other in ways
that have no need for
anything other than a
knowing nod or a con-
junctive squeeze
                    of the hand.

Mara's Lamp

For Anne, on our 37th
And for Nancy and Jerry Mara

1

Between the last sting
of the solstice sun
and the unstarred dark,
gripped centripetal
by Mara's hexagonic
hide-and-go-seek
streetlamp, we voyaged
our burgeoning bodies
into the shudder of shadow
and out to the moon-pulled
elixir of edges – let
them visit and estrange
till the *oh-li-oh-li-en-free*
sings us aback
to the home-post…

2

After 37 anniversaries
(so much already examined)
we reconnoitre like infant
archaeologists fingering
with solicitous touch
what is still most strange
and tenderly hedged,
knowing, even as we dare,
our love is as steadied and starred
as Mara's lamp.

Not Any Gift
An Un-Valentine Poem:

Sheaves of roses
stooked golden in
ersatz wintered
light will not do

(too often used to gild
your lover's guilt
or seal the wound of a
rued absence)

A Hallmark card
bobbing with hearts as
buoyant as the venerable
saint's pulled out and
offered undigested to
Jesus will not suffice

(our love in its bloom more
passionate than pilgrim
and in the cadenced elegy
of its ageing too domiciled
for the pink hyperboles
of rhymed romance)

And living as we now do
from room to arboured
room, breathing the same
nurtured silences / the
covert coincidence of
wink and conjugal
nudge, even a word too
edged or syllabic
could scribble the intimate
scansion of touch and just
caress
          between us.

So any gift of mine
(however emboxed as
Valentine or poesy),
any re-averral of our
love's long amaze,
must be transmuted
without rose or trope
thru the tender intoxication
of shared
         February
              days.

Small Gestures
A Birthday Poem for Anne

Thinking me fast asleep,
you plant a kiss upon
one arable cheek,
do not wait for any
break in the faithful
rhythm of my breathing –

a small gesture, perhaps,
but in it much abides:

>a room in Nuremburg,
>bridal-bright and un-
>dulant with sun-seethe
>and lovers in their morning
>urges…

>a speechless jog
>along some Huron dune
>or Georgian prospect:
>our hands deliberate/
>solo in the awkward
>afternoon – but, ah,
>the electric embrace
>of bodies consoling in the cottage dark…

or that evening (in our season
of evenings) when we forgot
to merely remember the
passion that presaged
and girder'd our lush
                      loving…

Later, dream-revived,
I ease up behind you
bent (ageless) over the
breakfast *Globe*
and lip-whisper a kiss
that is almost a word:

you do not turn
from the page, nor do
I expect you to.

Tears

For Anne. In loving memory
and for Katie and Rebecca

And you happiest amongst
your granddaughters, one
on either side (a triptych
Gainsborough would have adored)
on a chesterfield we bought
so many days ago,
where joy has abided in its royal
riches for fifty-seven
years, and it is harder to love
the world without you in it,
but you have given me girls
Heaven would be proud of
and so much more, and all
I can offer in return are these
tears.

The Point

For Anne
On Valentine's Day 2002

And you most at home
in fields fueled by flowers
and air loud with blue-
jays and bobolinks,
and random is your roaming
among blood-bright
poppies and marigolds
bronzed by bee-buzz,
the sun aflame in your hair
and milkweed-haze
silkens and hummingbirds
covet and Carolina
wrens anoint with song

(no wonder few can hear
your house-bound lover
proclaim, "I love you
in your element," or more
to the point
                "I love you")

Walking Together
On A Snowy Evening

Guelph, Ontario: January 1961
For Anne, on our 40th

In that first windfall winter
the evening snows nested
confessional on fluted limb
and bough (intimate as lovers'
fingers minting a caress),
their silence steepled our strolling
with mute music – we heeded
the hinting of hearts that had
no need for sense or season:
        enlinked, we grew abreast,
        waxed ecclesiastic
        at the blizzard-burst
        blessing our blood.

Urn

It isn't Grecian but its bronze
and pleasing curves are beyond
beautiful because all
that remains of you resides
inside that bevelled urn,
your last repose, so
close beside me
I can feel your love as it glows
the room golden, and when
I run my hand over its
slender tenderness, I see
your graceful face and look
for the hope you bring, brighter
than the light of a thousand dawns.

Love Itself

For Anne: Christmas 2001

I watch your hands in awe:
their filigree flair
on the chopping board,
the mothering moves they make
to soothe an infant's ache,
the way they coax roses
to illuminate a room,
the tints their instincts choose
to swatch and amaze a quilt,
their five-fingered grip
on a spade working the earth/
grooming its garden aglow,
and, ah, what strength they've drawn
from a thousand days of lending
grace to all they touched
with tenderness,
and when I hold them up
like this, as now I do,
love itself falls thru.

Locks

I fell in love with the carotene
curls you brandished like a badge
of honour: swept up
like a nun's wimple or let
fall as lush as Rapunzel's
locks: you took a simple
girl's delight in their evident
loveliness, and I adored
the woman who sported them
beyond reason and rhyme,
not knowing such love
would last a lifetime.

Whatever Grows

You were born with a green
thumb, and ever since
everything you've touched
has sprouted, budded or blossomed:
roses that tumble on their trellises,
petunia pots showering
our porch with a blaze of petals,
forget-me-nots
fringing the lawn with the
sprightliness of Spring:
you are a daughter of Demeter,
a dean of whatever
grows, and you are un-
amazed at your own delight

Kept Warm

For Anne: Valentine's Day 2007

The slow snows descend,
the knee-deep drifts
swallowing houses whole,
revising horizons,
the wind as thin and iced
as February's air:
we stroll the frozen land-
scape, hand in glove –
kept warm by love.

Endued

When you pulled up
in that brand-new
Volkswagon with the sun
roof, my heartbeat
abrupted, as the girl with the
clementine curls, a smile
festooned with freckles and a
glance that rhymed with romance
stepped into the autumnal light
in her lemon-yellow dress
and I was smitten breathless,
bitten by love's bite,
and needed no proof
for my endued delight or
my sublime obsession.

Patient

Tom and I spend
half a day fishing
on Cameron, baffled
by bass, spurned by even
the lowly perch, and so
it is a day of lassitude,
savouring the sun, and when
we putt up to Potsy's
dock, you are waiting
as patient as Penelope,
your eyes alight with love
and hopefulness, your smile
as wide as any horizon.

Marigold

Cameron Lake was our magical
place, where the sun bloomed
like a magnified marigold fully
ablaze, where the breeze off
the dimpled water feathered
our cheeks as we lazed on the
porch my uncle built
with his simple carpenter's craft,
and where the rooms were warmed
by wood-stove and the aroma
of weathered elm, in which
we tidied away the effortless
afternoons, perusing tomes
comic and tragic, and certain
that this was a home where love
abided.

For Anne

If you were a flower you'd be
a yellow rose sweetening
sunshine on June
afternoons, and at the edge
of evening mellowing moon-
light: we greet each
other in the morning's rise,
empowered by love in the
other's eyes, watching
as it grows and blooms
over the long years
we have been buoyantly
embowered.

Coupled

For a long time now
we have lain side by side,
coupled yet still distinct,
our bodies each folded
into its own furrow, close
enough to be tantalized
by touch, and if by chance
a hand should brush a hand,
it is a moment to be prized,
and when we wake,
with eyes enlinked,
our breathing in rhythmic rhyme,
what is exchanged in look
upon look will last
a lifetime.

A Birthday Poem

We have stopped counting
our birthdays, but the years
glide on without permission
or our say-so, but we have eased
into our age as gracefully
as Time and Earth allow
(your hand in my glove),
and whatever fears
we may have for the future
are flouted by our abiding love.

Cadenza

For Anne and our trips to Toronto:
Valentine's Day 2018

I try to curb my enthusiasm
as you sweep up to the curb
in your brand-new Volks,
you hair piled high
above the smile you flash me
with both of your Baltic blue
eyes, and when you step
down in your lilting lemon
dress, my breath is in
a frenzy, and I wonder what
god has blessed this day,
as we climb aboard and toddle
off to cadenza town.

Now You Are Gone

When lilacs bloom again
in all their lilting loveliness,
I'll think of you when daffodils
dazzle and tulips tantalize,
for there has always been
something of the Spring
in you with its perpetual
budding of hope and happiness,
even as our years lengthened,
and so, with summer gone
and Winter come a-chilling,
I need only recall
the lilacs in your eyes to find
the strength to carry on
and, above all, summon
the will to keep on loving.

Harmony

For Anne and for John Barnett, in memoriam

Some days before he died
Anne fetched her father
from the tedium of his nursing home,
put him in a taxi
(wheelchair and all)
and together they motored
back through the village
John had known for more
than half his life, each
house precisely familiar,
jogging memories as they flashed
by, and as soon as the Lake
came into view, they paused,
and easefully Anne manoeuvred
the chair down to the beach
and side by side they sat
and stared out at the
calming waters, father
and daughter locked
in mutual harmony,
sharing all that had passed
and what was left of their
                        future.

Towards The Light
For Anne: June 10, 1998

The years of our coming together
roll into each other like the brave
waves tumble upon my boyhood beach,
the air above them passionate with day-burst
they lust at with their just-about reaching.

Even then, I willed my bachelor being
to that circular foamed fury:
to be spun numb in my young bones
while the hurry of a hale heart
curves to quiet
          awake.

Even now, in the midst
of our eased intimacy
(our aging hours seasoned
with gesture and oblique delight)
I want to touch you everywhere
that's riotous with remembrance,
that's rollicking and Rubenesque
and stirred reminiscent
by waves
       arching
              towards light.

Part Three
Another Poem For Anne

These poems are for Anne,
in loving memory

Crimson

This sumac that has graced
our yard for these long
years is now in it death-
throes: once filigreed
with birds of every ilk
in their Sunday suits: robins
and sparrows, cardinals
and chickadees, and how
you loved to watch them flutter
down like fretful ballerinas
to the bowl of water you so
faithfully provided (and there
below the ruined trunk
new shoots tickle the air),
and see now its final burst
of bloom as if it did not
wish to say goodbye,
garnished-green leaves
hanging like shredded silk
that will for one last
time glow crimson
in the Fall, and how I wish
you could be there to hear
the hymn I will sing to you,
even though your going
has seared my soul.

Always

For the past few years
of our long-intertwined
history, we resided in distinct
floors, me above
in the study, inking poems
or perusing inch-thick
tomes, while you were happy
to grace the home rooms
with your perpetual presence,
your free spirit, your filigreed
flair, and I found some
comfort in imagining your love-
lined face, content to know
you were there, and assuming
you always would be.

Harvest

We were not Romeo and Juliet
with a balcony to keep us apart,
we began as companions, trotting
off together to Big
Town to take in La Boheme
or the Bolshoi: you suave
urbanite, me the country
bumpkin, but something
grew between us
other than our passion
for the arts, and in time we flew
with a single featherage under
a moon-piping sky,
and love bloomed like a
slow lily until we were doomed.
willy-nilly to harvest
our ripening hearts.

Epitaph

"Margaret Anne Gutteridge:
1935-2018": the simple
inscription on a granite plaque
in the tall-treed urn
garden, a triptych in cold
stone that will have to do
for a life lived between
that stiff brace of dates,
a life of joyous giving,
of self-effacement, enriched
by friends and family and days
of gratuitous grace in a world
often whittled to the bitten
bone: you will be remembered
long after the rains
have withered away the stark
reminder of our brief residence
here on Earth and memories
have begun to wobble, but lives
touched by such boldness
of being as yours will survive
in the hearts of those who loved you
until there are no more
hearts to throb.

Never Again

Never again will you sit
in front of the TV
cursing Trump and his candied
coif, your sense of fair
play outraged
by his demagogic gaffs,
his legion of lies that you,
who believed in truth with a
ruthless candor, despised
as we sat in tandem on the
chesterfield that served
two generations and watched
reality ruptured, loving
every minute because
our souls coupled. Never
again but still I wish
there was you and humpteen
Trumps.

Abiding

You once told me that you
decided not to be
a professional grandmother,
but Fate stepped in,
as she often does, with six
grandkids, and when
you cut your flowing locks
and let your hair curl up
into a frenzy of maternal red,
you took them underwing
like flocks of chicks in a feathered
hug, and oh how they tugged
at your hopeful heart until
you confessed your affection
and sang them cadenzas of
abiding love.

Our Love is More Potent

Your love unhinges
my heart, releases
the breath of my being;
in a world gone awry
your steadfastness
never ceases. which is why
as we edge towards Death
our love is more potent
than poetry while tinged
                      with regret.

On Honeymoon Bay

We make love under
a menstrual moon,
only the thin skin
of the tent between us,
the starlit dark
and the great aloneness
of the lake: we listen
to the rhythm of the waves echo
our own, and all we ask
is that the world in it stark
severity, for our sake, laughs
at lovers and lets their bodies
be.

They Say

They say that love is never
enough, but from the first
moment I spied you in that
vimming Volks with your un-
ruffled Rapunzellian hair
upswept in a tangerine burst
and those freckles like a spray
of Venusian stars upon
each cherished cheek
and those eyes blue
with sentient surprise,
I was smitten with Cupid's bent
bow and amorous arrow:
my fate thus already
written, and after all
what do "they" know?

Presence

I can't believe you're gone:
nothing prepares us
for the anguish of absence:
you filled your world with a
perpetual presence,
I still see you blooming
every room you graced,
every word I remember
hanging on in the long,
consummate conversation
of our life; your face will be
a potent palimpsest upon
my harrowed heart, and I am
consoled by the thought of our
lilting love, even
though my grief leaves
 me unmarrowed.

Urn

It isn't Grecian but its bronze
and pleasing curves are beyond
beautiful because all
that remains of you resides
inside that bevelled urn,
your last repose, so
close beside me
I can feel your love as it glows
the room golden, and when
I run my hand over its
slender tenderness, I see
your graceful face and look
for the hope you bring, brighter
than the light of a thousand
dawns.

Geyser

The day-lily is as steadfast
as Old Faithful's geysering
plume and when the dawn-light
lifts the bud's lid,
the petals, seething with sun,
open slowly like a Mozart
adagio, and by noon the bloom
has burst as bright as an orange
comet burrowing the night
sky, and you watched this
diurnal pantomime
and its lilting lustre and loved it
as much as I have loved
you, unbidden,
and, in your perpetual presence,
made a little bit wiser.

Miss Barnett

When I first laid eyes
upon Miss Barnett,
I observed a home-ec
teacher with an archipelago
of freckles and a burst of up-
surging tangerine locks,
patrolling the halls of Elmira
High with all the vim
of a school-marm, and little
did I know that we would
both be surprised by love
and its witting charm, and that
one of us would soon
be a missus.

Humble

You never cared much
for Heaven or its Holy Hope,
but the spirit that moved Jesus
to galvanize Galilee and bring
mercy into a numbed world
moved in you who exuded
such kindness, such
self-effacing grace,
who lavished love wherever
it was needed, who surprised us
with the ardor of your affection,
given so freely:
whom the gods extol
they first make humble.

Apart

In our latter aging years
we inhabited separate floors,
you below, me above,
and we greeted one another
each morning like two
old friends meeting
in Gibbons Park, and treasured
those few moments
we shared during our day–
light hours, but I could
gauge your measured presence
three doors away,
and knowing you were just
there was all that mattered:
it would take more than walls
to keep out hearts apart
or stall our levitating love.

Nurture

You always loved Spring
when purple crocuses coveted
the good ground recently
rinsed by rain, and you waited
patiently for a glimpse of the first
tulip shoots aereating the April
mornings, and then the budded
burst of our maple like baby's
fists clenching life
and their sudden exfoliation
showered us with shade,
and you breathed easier knowing
the world was coming back
with the salient sun, and soon
there would be daisies
and foxglove and I loved you
more for loving them:
your unquenchable nurturing urge
that made my heart sing.

Beatitude

Blessed are those who love
for they shall move mountains
and pacify the Seven Seas:
they are the ones who bring
each child out of itself
into the bright breeze
of the light, who nurture and nurse
and bind up the wounds
the world makes, who, like you,
do not rest until the last
suffering soul, above
or below, has come to loving
rest.

Prompt

I sat in the neighbouring room
and listened in fascination
as you prompted your pupils
into relinquishing their terror
of the printed page and those
letters tangling on their tongues,
but you knew all
the pedagogic angles and soothed
your charges into hinting at the
slippery syllables until
words were weighed and smoothed
tactical in those tender
minds, and you, no
rookie at this age-old
act, capped off
each lesson with a home-
made cookie.

Abrupt
After Emily Dickinson

Because you could not stop
for Death he kindly stopped
for you, making his solicitous
visit while you slept alone
(dreaming your last ecstatic
dream?) and interrupted
your thinning breath, while
the heart that loved the world
with all its flaws paused,
skipped a beat and stalled:
like your life, there was nothing
dramatic about your going:
you left us sleeping, peaceful,
mindful of the grief that would
surely seize us at your abrupt,
tender departure.

Eventually

When we were young and easy
in our own skin, we let
our bodies be as they pleased,
happy to find a home
in one another's arms,
and as we grew wiser
we met thigh to thigh
and our love sprung anew
with each familiar sigh,
and when age surprised
us out of the blue,
we let ourselves be
content to sit side by side
in abiding repose, knowing
that everything kith
and kin eventually goes.

Pendulum

My grief, like a pendulum,
comes and goes, the sight
of a yellow rose, emblem
of our long loving years,
can overwhelm or the chesterfield
where you lay during your last
days can amaze tears
I had thought forgotten,
but mostly it is the ghost
haunting these halls
above and below, but it's good
to mourn what we have lost,
for it tells us how far
love has come.

About the Author

Don Gutteridge is the author of more than fifty-five books: poetry, fiction and scholarly works in educational theory and practice. He was born in Sarnia, Ontario and raised in the nearby village of Point Edward. He graduated from Western with an Honours English degree, taught school for seven years and then joined Western's Faculty of Education. There he taught English methods for twenty-five years and is now Professor Emeritus. He won the 1972 UWO President's Medal for the best periodical poem of that year, "Death At Quebec." His poetry collection *Coppermine* was short-listed for the 1973 Governor General's Literary Award. To listen to interviews with the author, go to: http://thereandthen.podbean.com. Don lives in London, Ontario.

www.ingramcontent.com/pod-product-compliance
Lightning Source LLC
Chambersburg PA
CBHW020123130526
44591CB00032B/397